# ACTIVITY BOOK

# Santillana
# INTENSIVE
# English

## 5

Santillana USA

ISBN 1-58105-367-3 Activity Book 5

Santillana USA Publishing Company, Inc.
2105 N.W. 86th Avenue
Miami, FL 33122

# How to Use This Book

The goal of *Santillana Intensive English* (*SIE*) is to assist learners in acquiring communication skills as well as the academic language that is necessary to achieve in the all-English classroom.

Each grade-level of *SIE* is divided into 12 theme units. Each unit contains ten lessons found on individual Lesson Cards – 120 cards in each grade. To teach each lesson, the teacher need only follow the lesson plans on the Lesson Card. Each card uses a clear three-step approach: Teach, Practice and Apply, and Extend.

The goal of the *SIE* Activity Books is to reinforce the concepts, vocabulary, and language structures taught. The Home School Connection, an important part of every lesson, enables students to share their learning with family members. When finished, the Activity Book pages will serve as a permanent record of student achievement and may be incorporated into assessment portfolios.

The Activity Book tasks should be assigned after each lesson is completed. Students should complete them independently. The lessons may be completed in class or assigned for home-work. They should be corrected and returned to students. This procedure may be modified to handle the case of students at different stages of language acquisition in the same classroom. Following are brief descriptions of the stages of language acquisition (see Stephen D. Krashen, *The Natural Approach: Language Acquisition in the Classroom*, Upper Saddle River, NJ: Prentice Hall, 1996).

Stage 1, Preproduction
Learners have minimal or no comprehension of English. They may participate in activities by saying yes or no or by using gestures.

Stage 2, Early Production
Learners have some comprehension of English. They participate in activities by responding with single words or short phrases in English.

Stage 3, Speech Emergence
Learners participate in activities by responding with longer phrases and complete sentences. They can engage in conversation, narrate events, and express opinions.

Stage 4, Intermediate Fluency
Learners can deal with a wider variety of topics in conversation, can speak extemporaneously, and can manipulate shades of meaning.

The following chart compares the Activity Book tasks with learners at the four stages of language acquisition. The filled-in boxes indicate that those learners can do those tasks.

|  | fill-in | label (labels given) | match | write sentence | draw | label (labels not given) | write paragraph |
|---|---|---|---|---|---|---|---|
| Preproduction |  |  |  |  |  |  |  |
| Early Production |  |  |  |  |  |  |  |
| Speech Emergence |  |  |  |  |  |  |  |
| Intermediate Fluency |  |  |  |  |  |  |  |

The tasks that are most challenging for Preproduction and Early Production learners are writing sentences and paragraphs. Students at those stages can still participate in these writing activities if some oral preparation is done in class and they work in pairs with students at a higher stage of language acquisition. Oral preparation might include a discussion of the subject, writing the key words on the board for students to copy and learn, and providing oral and written examples. The lower-level learner might begin by copying the correct work of a more proficient partner but should be encouraged to produce original writing as well. As the academic year progresses, less pair work should be necessary. If more proficient students are not available to work with the lower-level students, adult or student tutors or the classroom teacher may be asked to work with them.

The Home School Connection activity may also be utilized by adult or student tutors to help move learners at the Speech Emergence and Intermediate Fluency stages to higher levels of proficiency. The tutor should be asked to participate as if he or she were the family member. The learner can practice the task several times if necessary before attempting it with a family member.

In all these ways, the *SIE* Activity Books contribute to the overall program goal of mastery of social and academic English in record time.

My name is _____ .

She is a _____ .    He is a _____ .    He is the _____ .

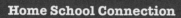

**Use these words to label the people and places at school.**

| | | | |
|---|---|---|---|
| cafeteria | librarian | playground | secretary |
| crossing guard | janitor | principal | teacher |

**Write the correct phrase from the box below under the picture.**

> get in line　　　 hello　　　 raise your hand
> sit down　　　 stand up　　　 work with

_____

_____

_____

_____

_____

_____

**Home School Connection**

Have students demonstrate each action and repeat appropriate phrases for family members. Encourage them to ask family members to participate in giving and responding to commands.

**Write the correct word from the box below under the picture.**

cafeteria            library
classroom            office

**Complete the sentence by writing the correct word in the blank.**

1. The principal is in the _____ .

2. We eat in the _____ .

3. Books are in the _____ .

4. Our teacher is in the _____ .

**Home School Connection**

Encourage students to share their work at home. If possible, a family member should read the sentence completion orally so the student can respond orally.

**Write the correct word or words from the box below under the picture.**

| basketball | softball | slide |
|---|---|---|
| soccer ball | basketball hoop | swing |

_____

_____

_____

_____

_____

_____

**Write the correct word on the line.**

1. We play _____ with a bat and a ball.

2. We shoot hoops with a _____ .

3. We kick the ball on a _____ field.

**Connect each word to its matching picture.**

drinking fountain

straw

milk

napkin

fork

knife

spoon

table

bench

trashcan

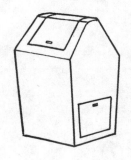

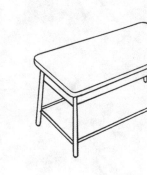

1. These are the things we find in the _____ .

2. We eat our _____ in the cafeteria.

**Home School Connection**

Encourage students to help set the table at home, repeating the names of the utensils and dishes for a family member.

**Write a word in each blank space so that the sentence tells about the picture.**

1. We are in the room for _____ _____ .
2. We go _____ to study, speak and write.

1. We are on the playground for _____ .
2. This comes after _____ _____ .
3. We go _____ for this.

1. We eat in the _____ .
2. This comes after _____ _____ .
3. We go _____ for this.

**Connect each word to its matching picture. Then, beneath each picture, write a sentence about that picture.**

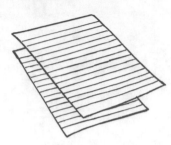

pen

pencil

ruler

paper

textbook

computer

desk

chair

bookcase

chalkboard

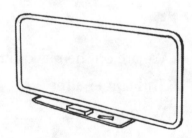

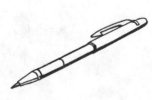

1. These are the things we find in the _____ .

2. Another person we find in the classroom is our _____ .

**Home School Connection**

Ask students to draw a picture of their classroom, incorporating as many of the objects from the above list as possible. Encourage them to share their drawing with a family member, naming each object that appears in the drawing.

**Connect each word to its matching picture.**

$+$

$\times$

$=$

addition
division
multiplication
ruler
subtraction
fraction
equal
number
problem

$-$

37

$4 + 1 =$

$\frac{1}{4}$

$\div$

1. These are the things I find in _____ .

2. When I complete a problem, I should _____ _____ _____ .

**Home School Connection**

Ask students to share some of their work in mathematics and describe the operations and computation on their page, using as many of the above vocabulary words as possible.

**Write the correct word or phrase from the box below under the picture.**

| upper case letter | question mark | comma |
| --- | --- | --- |
| lower case letter | period | sentence |

G

_____

,

_____

We went home.

_____

g

_____

?

_____

.

_____

**Home School Connection**

Have students take home a textbook or paper they have written and identify the symbols and terms for a family member. Students should ask the family member to quiz them on the symbols and terms.

# Name

---

**Name**

**Write the correct word from the box below to complete the sentence under the picture.**

> animals      buildings      weather
> plants      water      people

_____ is a part of our environment.

_____ are a part of our environment.

_____ are a part of our environment.

_____ is a part of our environment.

_____ are a part of our environment.

_____ are a part of our environment.

| | | |
|---|---|---|
| school | teacher | classroom |
| janitor | office | cafeteria | students |
| secretary | playground | principal |

## Use the words in the box and other words you know to complete the sentences correctly.

1. The name of my school is _____ .

2. My classroom is number _____ .

3. My teacher's name is _____ .

4. The _____ works in the office.

5. Another person who works in the office is the _____ .

6. The _____ helps keep the school clean.

7. We play games on the _____ .

8. There are many _____ at school.

9. We eat lunch in the _____ .

10. My _____ helps me in the classroom.

11. There are students and a teacher in my _____ .

12. The principal and secretary work in the _____ .

13. I go to _____ to learn.

**Home School Connection**

Ask students to share the information about their school, naming the individuals found there. Encourage students to ask a family member to name an individual's position (such as *principal*) and allow the student to supply the person's name.

**Name**

## Write the correct word from the box under each picture.

| house | mobile home | bedroom |
| apartment | kitchen | bathroom |

_____

_____

_____

_____

_____

_____

## Write the correct word on the line.

1. I sleep in a _____ .

2. I eat in the _____ .

3. I take a bath in the _____ .

**Use the words from the box to label the picture.**

| | | | |
|---|---|---|---|
| street | video store | corner | bakery |
| stop sign | barbershop | grocery store | signal |

Encourage students to take a walk with a family member, naming the things they see on the walk. You may wish to suggest an "I Spy" format for the walk.

**Use the words from the box to label the picture.**

| | | | |
|---|---|---|---|
| gas station | library | fire department | post office |
| movie theater | | supermarket | park |
| police station | school | restaurant | hospital |

**Home School Connection**

Encourage students to take a more extensive walk with a family member, naming the things they see on the walk. You may wish to suggest an "I Spy" format for the walk.

**Name**

## Write the correct word from the box under each picture.

| police officer | letter carrier | nurse |
| dentist | fire fighter | doctor |

_____

_____

_____

_____

_____

_____

## Write the correct word on the line.

1. A _____ _____ brings me the mail.
2. A _____ helps me keep my teeth clean.
3. A _____ helps me if I am sick.

**Use the words from the box to label the picture.**

restaurant          playground          amusement park
movie theater          park          skating rink

**Home School Connection**

Encourage students to look through magazines, newspapers, or books with a family member, finding examples of fun places in their community. They should label each site orally.

Name

**Write the correct word from the box under each picture.**

> beach        lake        mountain
>     river        park            mall

_____

_____

_____

_____

_____

_____

**Write a sentence about some of the special places in your community.**

_____

_____

**Name**

Color the state where you live red. Write the name of your state on the map. Label the compass rose on the map with North, South, East, and West.

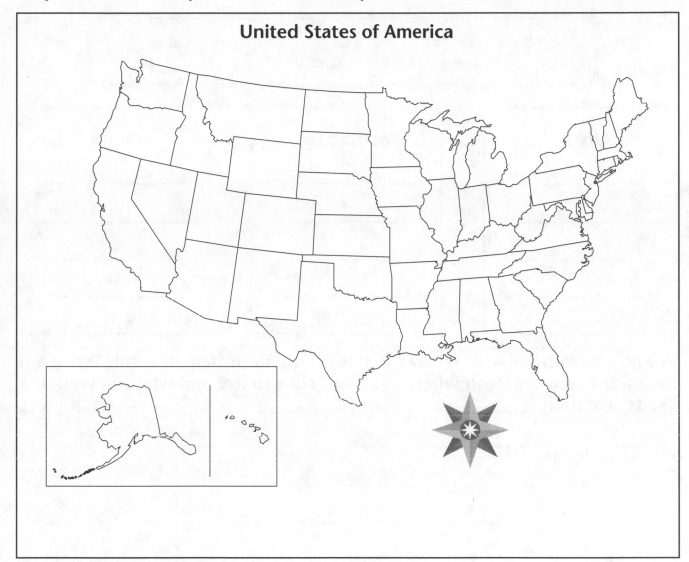

**United States of America**

**Complete the sentences below.**

1. I live in the state of _____ .

2. The city or town where I live is _____ .

4. Our state flower is the _____ .

5. Our state tree is the _____ .

**Home School Connection**  Have students share their map with a family member and together label as many of the states other than their own as possible.

**Name** _____

**Write the words from the box in the correct category. You may use each word more than one time.**

| bike | bus | car |
|------|-----|-----|
| horse | taxi | train |

| **Urban** | **Suburban** | **Rural** |
|-----------|--------------|-----------|
| _____ | _____ | _____ |
| _____ | _____ | _____ |
| _____ | _____ | _____ |
| _____ | _____ | _____ |

**Would you rather live in an area that is urban, suburban, or rural? Write a paragraph below telling where you would like to live and why you would like to live there.**

_____

_____

_____

_____

_____

_____

_____

**Home School Connection**   Have students ask a family member about other places they may have lived. Have them ask where they would like to live and why.

**Write a sentence about people in the United States of America for each word or phrase below.**

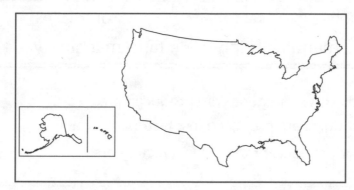

immigrant

1. _____

melting pot

2. _____

state

3. _____

nation

4. _____

ranch

5. _____

custom

6. _____

border

7. _____

language

8. _____

**Name**

## Use the words in the box to fill in the blanks in each line.

| | | | |
|---|---|---|---|
| conveyor belt | factory | automobiles | airplanes |
| computers | manufacturing | farm machinery | clothes |

1. A building or buildings where goods are produced is called a _____ .

2. When goods or products are produced in a factory, we call it _____ .

3. Five of the goods or products produced in a factory are _____ , _____ , _____ , _____ ,
   and _____ .

4. A _____ carries parts and products to places in the factory.

## Write a sentence using each word in the box.

1. _____

   _____

2. _____

   _____

3. _____

   _____

4. _____

   _____

5. _____

   _____

6. _____

   _____

7. _____

   _____

8. _____

   _____

**Home School Connection**     Have students describe what they know about factories and manufacturing to a family member.

**Use the words from the box to label the picture.**

| plow | barn | cow | horse |
|---|---|---|---|
| pig | chicken | farmer | |
| sheep | hay | tractor | silo |

## Use the words from the box to label the picture.

| | | |
|---|---|---|
| | building | hammer | hard hat |
| saw | shovel | architect |
| | drill | screwdriver | plans |

**Use the words in the box to fill in the blank lines.**

> janitor      bus driver      teacher
> cafeteria worker      librarian      nurse
> secretary      coach      principal
> professor      superintendent      college

1. A _____ is a person who helps students learn.

2. A teacher at a college is called a _____ .

3. A person who helps keep the school clean and safe is a _____ .

4. A _____ prepares lunch for us at school.

5. A person who takes care of the books in the school library is the _____ .

6. The _____ is the person in charge of the school.

7. A person who may watch out for your health at school is a _____ .

8. A _____ works in the school office.

9. The person who helps get you to school on a bus is a _____ .

10. A _____ helps students on sports teams.

11. A _____ makes decisions for a whole school system.

12. After elementary school, middle school, and high school, you might go to _____ .

Name

**Use the words in the box to fill in the blank lines.**

> ambulance      nurse      hospital      paramedic
> dentist      scientist      stethoscope
> medicine      doctor      clinic      treatment

1. A _____ treats injuries and tries to help people get well.

2. A person who helps you take care of your teeth is a _____ .

3. If you are very sick, you may have to go to stay in a _____ .

4. A _____ takes care of people on their way to the hospital in an ambulance.

5. A person who takes care of people in a hospital or doctor's office is a _____ .

6. A person who studies one area of science is a _____ .

7. A doctor or nurse may use a _____ to listen to your heart beat.

8. An _____ is a vehicle that takes sick or wounded people to hospitals.

9. Some doctors have an office in a _____ .

10. A doctor who is helping you to get well has a _____ for your illness or injury.

11. Doctors study _____ .

**On the lines below, write a short paragraph describing how you felt when you were last sick.**

_____

_____

_____

_____

_____

_____

**Home School Connection**

Have students describe the different medical careers on this page to a family member.

Write the correct name below the picture of each community worker.

| police officer | fire fighter | letter carrier |
| store clerk | waitress | mechanic |

_____

_____

_____

_____

_____

_____

**Home School Connection**

Have students interview a family member to jointly create a list of other jobs in the community. Students should share their lists with the class.

**Name**

**Write a sentence using each word or phrase above the sentence line that tells about people who work in the arts and entertainment.**

musician
1. _____

_____

dancer
2. _____

_____

disc jockey
3. _____

_____

illustrator
4. _____

_____

actor
5. _____

_____

actress
6. _____

_____

camera operator
7. _____

_____

**Home School Connection**

Encourage students to explain these jobs in arts and entertainment to a family member.

**Write a sentence that answers the question above each numbered line.**

What does "the future" mean?

1. _____

_____

_____

What does the term "next generation" mean?

2. _____

_____

_____

Where do you think you might be living in ten years?

3. _____

_____

_____

What do you think you might want to be?

4. _____

_____

_____

What can you do now to get ready to become a responsible adult?

5. _____

_____

_____

**Home School Connection**    Encourage students to share their sentences as well as their opinions with a family member.

**Write a sentence that describes each word above the line.**

club

1. _____

_____

_____

organization

2. _____

_____

_____

committee

3. _____

_____

_____

group

4. _____

_____

_____

volunteer

5. _____

_____

_____

**Home School Connection**

Encourage students to share their sentences as well as what they have learned about people working together with a family member.

Color the state where you live blue. Write the name of your state on the
map. Label the compass rose on the map with North, South, East, and West.

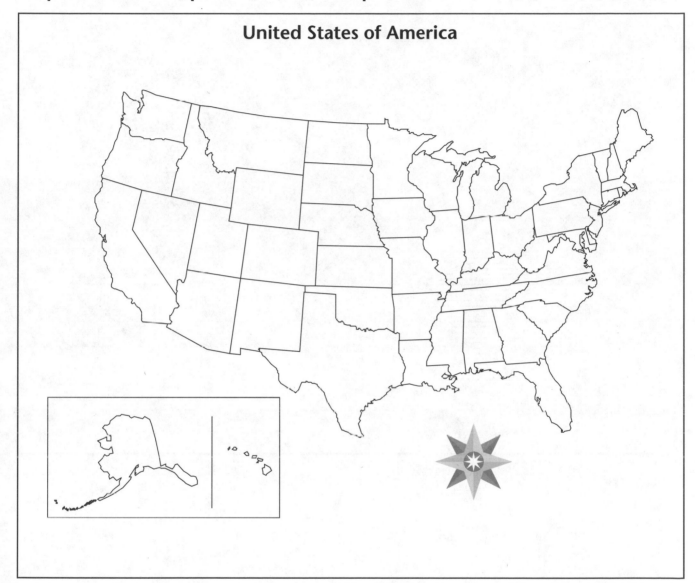

**United States of America**

## Complete the sentences below.

1. I live in the state of _____ .

2. The city or town where I live is _____ .

3. My state is beside _____ .

**On the map below, write the name of each continent where it should appear.**

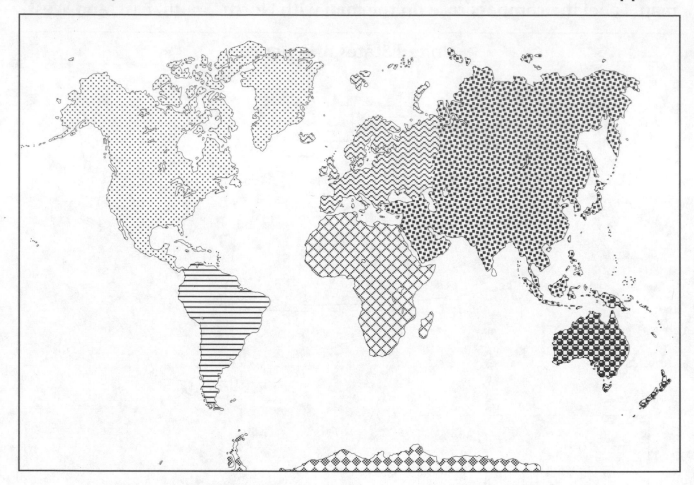

Each of the words in the box is about something from the Earth's oceans. Connect the word in the box to its matching picture. Then, beneath each picture, write a sentence about that picture.

_____

_____

dolphin
fish
starfish
whale
seaweed
shark

_____

_____

_____

_____

**Home School Connection**

Encourage students to share the information they have about ocean life with a family member, naming the sea life on this page as well as any other sea life they may recall.

**Write a sentence using each word or phrase above the sentence line that tells about life on Earth's rivers.**

river

1. _____

_____

riverboat

2. _____

_____

bank

3. _____

_____

current

4. _____

_____

recreation

5. _____

_____

tributary

6. _____

_____

wildlife

7. _____

_____

**Home School Connection**

Encourage students to share and explain their sentences about life on a river to a family member.

**Write a sentence that tells about a desert using each word below.**

sand

1. _____

oasis

2. _____

temperature

3. _____

hot

4. _____

water

5. _____

climate

6. _____

wind

7. _____

moisture

8. _____

**Each of the words in the box is about forests. Connect the word in the box to its matching picture. Then, beneath each picture, write a sentence about that picture.**

_____

_____

wildlife
forest ranger
lumber
plant
tree
fire

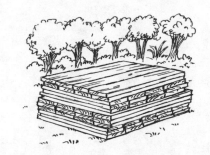

_____

_____

_____

_____

**Home School Connection**

Encourage students to share the information they have about forest life with a family member, naming the things on this page as well as any other features of forest life they may recall.

**Use the words in the box to fill in the blank lines.**

| hot | vegetation | forest |
|---|---|---|
| tropical | equator | wildlife |

1. A rain forest is a dense evergreen _____ .
2. Almost all rain forests are in _____ regions.
3. The climate in a rain forest is _____ and wet.
4. Many rain forests are found close to the _____ .
5. When trees are cut down for lumber, much of the rain forest's _____ loses its home.
6. Many different kinds of plants and other kinds of _____ grow in the rain forest.

**Write a paragraph to describe what you think life would be like in a rain forest.**

_____

_____

_____

_____

_____

_____

_____

_____

_____

_____

**Home School Connection**

Have students read their sentences and paragraphs to a family member. Then, have them ask family members to share what they may know about rain forests.

Name

In the space below, create a drawing of the tundra. Include in your drawing all of the words listed in the box.

| polar bear | hawk | reindeer |
|---|---|---|
| walrus | moss | permafrost |

Write a sentence for each word.

grassland

1. _____

prairie

2. _____

plains

3. _____

temperate

4. _____

bison

5. _____

drought

6. _____

rainfall

7. _____

wheat

8. _____

**Home School Connection**

Have students create a drawing of a grassland scene. Encourage them to ask a family member to help them label the objects they have put into the scene.

**Write a sentence for each word.**

wetland

1. _____

mud flat

2. _____

marsh

3. _____

bog

4. _____

decay

5. _____

swamp

6. _____

habitat

7. _____

coast

8. _____

**Home School Connection**   Have students describe some of the characteristics of a wetland to a family member.

On the map below, write the names of the two North American mountain ranges where they should appear. Use colored markers or crayons to indicate the mountains.

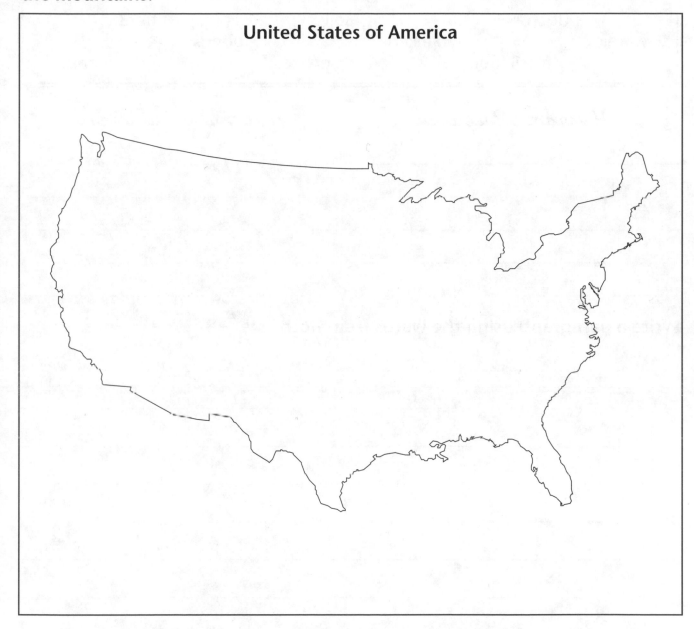

**United States of America**

Appalachian Mountains          Rocky Mountains

**Write the words from the box in the correct list. Each word will fit into either Human Resources or Natural Resources.**

| | | | |
|---|---|---|---|
| doctor | | soil | trees |
| water | banker | | goods |
| fossil fuel | | services | land |

*Human Resources*

_____
_____
_____
_____

*Natural Resources*

_____
_____
_____
_____

**Write a paragraph using the words from both lists.**

_____
_____
_____
_____
_____
_____
_____
_____

**Home School Connection**

Encourage students to discuss the differences between Natural Resources and Human Resources with a family member, coming up with an additional list of two more items in each category.

# Write a sentence for each word.

Color the Midwest and Great Plains region green.
Color the Mountain West orange.
Color the Southwest pink.
Color the Southeast red.
Color the Mid-Atlantic yellow.
Color New England blue.
Color the Pacific West purple.

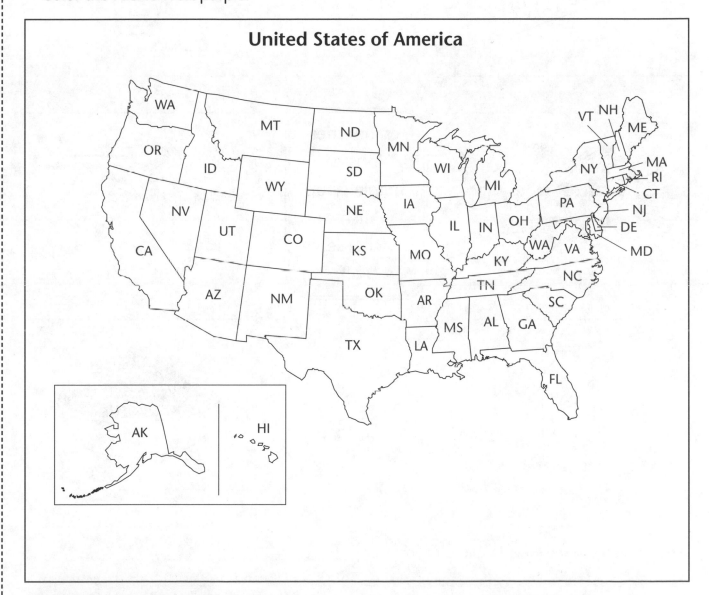

United States of America

**Each of the words in the box tells about a product from New England. Connect the word in the box to its matching picture. Then, beneath each picture, write a sentence about that picture.**

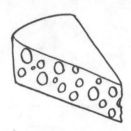

_____

_____

cranberries
lobster
maple syrup
fish
cheese
milk

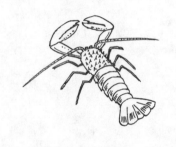

_____

_____

_____

_____

The six states in the New England region are _____ , _____ ,
_____ , _____ , _____ , and _____ .

**Name** _____

Each of the words in the box tells about a product from the Middle Atlantic. Connect the word in the box to its matching picture. Then, beneath each picture, write a sentence about that picture.

_____
_____

_____
_____

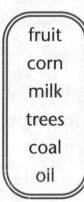

fruit
corn
milk
trees
coal
oil

_____
_____

_____
_____

_____
_____

_____
_____

The five states in the Middle Atlantic region are _____ , _____ , _____ , _____ , and _____ .

**Home School Connection**

Encourage students to share the information they have about the Middle Atlantic region with a family member.

Each of the words in the box tells about a product from the Southeast. Connect the word in the box to its matching picture. Then, beneath each picture, write a sentence about that picture.

_____

_____

_____

_____

oil
cotton
textiles
peanuts
oranges
coal

_____

_____

_____

_____

_____

_____

_____

_____

The twelve states in the Southeast region are _____ , _____ , _____ , _____ , _____ , _____ , _____ , _____ , _____ , _____ , _____ , and _____ .

**Home School Connection**　Encourage students to share the information they have about the Southeast region with a family member.

Each of the words in the box tells about a product from the Midwest and Great Plains region. Connect the word in the box to its matching picture. Then, beneath each picture, write a sentence about that picture.

_____

_____

_____

_____

apples
corn
vegetables
wheat
automobiles
meat

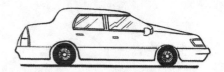

_____

_____

_____

_____

_____

_____

The twelve states in the Midwest and Great Plains region are _____ , _____ , _____ , _____ , _____ , _____ , _____ , _____ , _____ , _____ , _____ , and _____ .

Each of the words in the box tells about a product from the Southwest region. Connect the word in the box to its matching picture. Then, beneath each picture, write a sentence about that picture.

_____

_____

_____

_____

```
wheat
cotton
cattle
citrus fruit
peppers
oil
```

_____

_____

_____

_____

_____

_____

_____

_____

_____

_____

The four states in the Southwest region are _____ , _____ ,

_____ , and _____ .

**Home School Connection**

Encourage students to share the information they have about the Southwest region with a family member.

Each of the words in the box tells about a product from the Mountain West region. Connect the word in the box to its matching picture. Then, beneath each picture, write a sentence about that picture.

_____

_____

_____

_____

cattle
sheep
oil
trees
minerals

_____

_____

_____

_____

_____

_____

The six states in the Mountain West region are _____ , _____ ,
_____ , _____ , _____ , and _____ .

**Home School Connection**

Encourage students to share the information they have about the Mountain West region with a family member.

Each of the words in the box tells about a product from the Pacific West region. Connect the word in the box to its matching picture. Then, beneath each picture, write a sentence about that picture.

_____

_____

_____

_____

| fish |
| cattle |
| wheat |
| fruit |
| oil |
| trees |

_____

_____

_____

_____

_____

_____

_____

_____

The five states in the Pacific West region are _____ , _____ , _____ , _____ , and _____ .

**Write a sentence for each word or phrase.**

Asia

1. _____

North America

2. _____

South America

3. _____

Arctic Ocean

4. _____

Bering Strait

5. _____

land bridge

6. _____

migration

7. _____

nomad

8. _____

Pacific Ocean

9. _____

continent

10. _____

**Use the words in the box to fill in the blank lines.**

| | |
|---|---|
| time line | Spain      Asia |
| Europe | ship      spices |

1. Long ago, people who lived in Europe traded with people who lived in _____.

2. They traded for _____ that would make their food taste better and last longer.

3. It took a long time for people who lived in _____ to travel overland to Asia.

4. Christopher Columbus thought he could sail a _____ east and reach Asia.

5. Christopher Columbus sailed from _____ in 1492.

6. A _____ tells the order things happened.

**Write a paragraph to describe what you think Christopher Columbus's voyage was like.**

_____

_____

_____

_____

_____

_____

_____

_____

_____

_____

**Home School Connection**      Have students read their sentences and paragraphs to a family member.

**Use the words in the box to fill in the blank lines.**

temples          astronomy          aqueduct

empire          cities          civilization

Three great civilizations lived in Central and South America long before the explorers came to the new world.

The Maya _____ lived in Mexico and Guatemala more than 1,500 years ago. The Maya grew and stored corn. They were wonderful artists. They made beautiful pottery, statues, and jewelry and made a system of writing. They built more than 40 _____ .

The Incas settled along the western coast of South America. They built an _____ system to carry water to their crops. They built roads and bridges for over 2,000 miles. They carved great blocks of stone to build homes and _____ .

The Aztecs settled in central Mexico. Their _____ had over 10 million people in a number of cities. They built roads, canals, and aqueducts. They were traders and studied _____ . They could set broken bones, fill cavities in teeth, and could even do brain surgery.

**Select one of the three great civilizations – the Mayas, the Incas, or the Aztecs. Write a paragraph about what you think life would have been like if you had lived in that civilization.**

_____

_____

_____

_____

_____

_____

**Home School Connection**          Have students read their paragraphs to a family member.

**Write a sentence using each word or phrase above the sentence line that tells about the early settlements.**

beaver, otter, and other furs

1. _____

gold

2. _____

colony

3. _____

Dutch

4. _____

English

5. _____

French

6. _____

mission

7. _____

settlement

8. _____

Spanish

9. _____

settler

10. _____

**Home School Connection**

Have students create a drawing of what they think one of the early settlements might have looked like. Have them share their drawing with a family member, explaining how the settlement worked.

Name

**Use the words in the box to fill in the blank lines.**

| | | | |
|---|---|---|---|
| religious freedom | beans | settlers | Puritans |
| Mayflower | corn | Thanksgiving | Native Americans |

Pilgrims and _____ started the first colonies in New England. They left England because they wanted _____ . They sailed on a ship called the _____ in 1620.

Most of the early settlers were farmers. They learned how to plant _____ and _____ from the friendly Native Americans. The settlers cut down tall trees in the forest. They caught many fish from the sea. Fish and trees were sent back to England in exchange for the goods that the _____ could not make themselves.

In celebration for making it through their first year, they held a harvest festival with the _____ . Today, this celebration is known as _____ .

**Write a paragraph about what you think life might have been like in the New England colonies.**

_____
_____
_____
_____
_____
_____
_____
_____
_____

**Home School Connection**   Have students read their paragraphs to a family member.

**Name**

**Use the words in the box to fill in the blank lines.**

> Africa      tobacco      slaves
>
> colony      cotton      cash crop

The Southern Colonies were Virginia, Maryland, North Carolina, South Carolina, and Georgia. Life in Jamestown in the Virginia colony was hard at first, but more people arrived from England with food. Jamestown was the first successful English _____ .

The settlers learned that _____ would grow in Virginia. Tobacco became popular in Europe. It became an important _____ for the planters in the colony. The planters needed more workers to grow this crop, so they captured people from _____ , made them slaves and brought them to Virginia. More than 600,000 _____ were brought to America from Africa. The slaves worked in the fields and picked _____ , tobacco, and other crops. They also waited on the people who owned them.

**Write a paragraph about what you think life might have been like in the Southern Colonies.**

_____

_____

_____

_____

_____

_____

_____

_____

**Home School Connection**      Have students read their paragraphs to a family member.

**Use the words in the box to fill in the blank lines.**

> prosperous         New York         treaty
> William Penn      advertise      Pennsylvania

King Charles II of England gave _____ the right to start a colony in America. Penn named the colony Pennsylvania in honor of his father. He wrote letters to _____ the life Pennsylvania had to offer. These advertisements convinced people to come to the Middle Colonies to live. Thousands of European settlers sailed from Europe and settled in _____ , _____ , and New Jersey. William Penn believed that the Native American people were the true owners of the land that the king had given him. He made a _____ , or agreement, with the Lenape tribe. Pennsylvania became a peaceful and _____ colony.

**Write a paragraph about what you think life might have been like in the Middle Colonies.**

_____

_____

_____

_____

_____

_____

_____

_____

_____

_____

_____

**Home School Connection**      Have students read their paragraphs to a family member.

Name _____

**Use the words in the box to fill in the blank lines.**

| | | |
|---|---|---|
| independent | Great Britain | taxes |
| colonies | Revolutionary War | patriots |

The American _____ had been part of Great Britain for a long time. They looked on George III as their king. But the king began doing things that were making the colonists angry. The kind said they could not move farther to the west into the lands of the Native Americans. He said the colonists had to pay more _____ . They could not agree. So, in 1776 a group of American _____ decided to break away from _____ and declare the independence of the American colonies. They wanted the colonies to be a separate nation. The king did not agree, so the _____ , or war for independence, began. It lasted for eight years. Finally, the British army surrendered and Great Britain agreed that its colonies were now free and _____ .

**Write a paragraph about what you think it might have been like to be a patriot in the Revolutionary War.**

_____

_____

_____

_____

_____

_____

_____

_____

_____

_____

**Home School Connection**     Have students read their paragraphs to a family member.

**Write a sentence using each word or phrase that tells about the new nation – the United States of America.**

Constitutional Convention

1. _____

delegate

2. _____

document

3. _____

constitution

4. _____

laws

5. _____

rules

6. _____

Philadelphia

7. _____

government

8. _____

representative

9. _____

state

10. _____

# Use the words in the puzzle to complete the sentences below.

```
J                 C O N S T I T U T I O N
U                 O
D                 N
I                 G
C                 R
I                 E
A                 
L E G I S L A T I V E
        S         X
              P R E S I D E N T
                  C
                  U
S U P R E M E C O U R T
                  I
                  V
                  E
```

1. The branch of government that makes the laws is called the _____ Branch.

2. The branch of government that carries out the laws is the _____ Branch.

3. The branch of government that decides what the laws mean is the _____ Branch.

4. The _____ is the head of the Executive Branch.

5. There are two parts to the Legislative Branch – the Senate, and the House of Representatives – that make up what is called _____ .

6. The Judicial Branch of our national government is called the _____ .

7. The highest law in our country is the _____ .

**Home School Connection**    Have students research with a family member the names of their senators and representatives to the United States government.

The United States began to change and grow almost as soon as it became a nation. The words and sentences below are about the westward expansion of the United States. Use the words in the box to fill in the blank lines.

| | |
|---|---|
| Lewis and Clark | President Jefferson |
| Louisiana Purchase | canoe | Sacajawea |

1. The land the United States bought that was west of the Mississippi River was called the

   _____ .

2. _____ sent out an expedition to learn more about the territory.

3. The explorers who led the expedition were _____ .

4. They were led by a Native American guide named _____ .

5. The explorers went up the Missouri River in a _____ .

**Write a paragraph about what you think it might have been like to be an explorer learning about the Louisiana Purchase for the first time.**

_____

_____

_____

_____

_____

_____

_____

_____

_____

_____

**Home School Connection**    Have students read their paragraphs to a family member.

**Name**

**The Industrial Revolution was a time of new inventions and machines. The words and sentences below are about the Industrial Revolution. Use the words in the box to fill in the blank lines in the sentences.**

| | | |
|---|---|---|
| mass-produce | steamboat | telegraph |
| locomotive | textile mills | |

1. Robert Fulton built a _____ that improved river travel.

2. Peter Cooper built a _____ that made land travel much faster.

3. The invention of the _____ let people communicate with each other from very far away.

4. Factories where cloth was made were called _____ .

5. Machines helped factories _____ goods.

**Draw a picture of either a steamboat on a river or a locomotive traveling the railroad. Be sure to give your drawing a title.**

**Write a sentence using each word or phrase that tells about the American journey to the Civil War.**

cotton

1. _____

abolitionist

2. _____

Cuba, Canada, Mexico, and the Bahamas

3. _____

freedom

4. _____

Underground Railroad

5. _____

slavery

6. _____

escape

7. _____

oppose

8. _____

fields

9. _____

enslaved people

10. _____

**Home School Connection**     Have students create a drawing of one of the stops on the Underground Railroad. Encourage them to share their drawing with a family member.

**The question of slavery divided America. States in the South began to secede from the United States. Write a paragraph about this unhappy time in American history using the words in the box below.**

| | | | |
|---|---|---|---|
| Civil War | secede | Confederacy | Union |
| Emancipation Proclamation | | battle | Abraham Lincoln |

_____

_____

_____

_____

_____

_____

_____

_____

_____

_____

_____

_____

_____

_____

_____

In the box below there are six words. Three of these words were things that were important to Native Americans. The other three words were things important to homesteaders and miners. Write the words in the list where they belong. After each list, write a short paragraph that tells why these things were important to each group.

| buffalo | teepee | gold |
|---|---|---|
| railroad | prairie land | silver |

*Native Americans*

_____

_____

_____

*Homesteaders and Miners*

_____

_____

_____

*These things were important to the Native Americans because*

_____

_____

_____

_____

*These things were important to the homesteaders and miners*

*because* _____

_____

_____

_____

**Home School Connection**

Have students explain to a family member the conflict between the Native Americans and those individuals who wanted to expand to the Western Frontier.

Name

Many inventions changed the lives of people. Some of these early inventions were the phonograph, the telephone, the train, and the typewriter. Read the word in each box. Draw a picture of the old-time version of each invention. Write a sentence below each picture that tells about your drawing.

| | |
|---|---|
| phonograph | telephone |

| | |
|---|---|
| train | typewriter |

**Home School Connection**

Ask students to describe to a family member the early inventions above. Then, have them discuss the changes that each has gone through, leading to the versions we have today.

**America has always been a country of immigrants. Write a sentence about this country of immigrants by using each of the words or phrases.**

Statue of Liberty

1. _____

immigration

2. _____

melting pot

3. _____

ancestor

4. _____

customs

5. _____

native-born

6. _____

urban

7. _____

immigrant

8. _____

quota

9. _____

tenement

10. _____

**Name**

After America explored the west, many people were happy to improve America's cities and farmlands and keep to themselves. They were called Isolationists. Other explorers, business people, and politicians were still looking for opportunities to add more territory or own colonies. These people were called Imperialists. Write several paragraphs that tell whether you would prefer to have been an Isolationist or an Imperialist. Be sure to tell why you would have made that choice.

_____

_____

_____

_____

_____

_____

_____

_____

_____

_____

_____

_____

_____

_____

_____

_____

**Home School Connection**

Encourage students to share their paragraphs as well as their reasoning with a family member.

World War I started in Europe in 1914. The Allied Powers began to fight against the Central Powers. Use what you have learned and list the countries listed in the box under the correct heading.

| Great Britain | Austria-Hungary | Germany |
| Ottoman Empire | France | Belgium | Russia |

**Allied Powers**

_____

_____

_____

**Central Powers**

_____

_____

_____

Write a paragraph that tells what happened when the United States of America joined in the war on the side of the Allied Powers.

_____

_____

_____

_____

_____

_____

_____

**Name**

## Write a sentence using each word or phrase that tells about the changes World War I made in America.

factory

1. _____

civilian

2. _____

conserve

3. _____

Great Migration

4. _____

migrant

5. _____

patriotism

6. _____

replacement

7. _____

resources

8. _____

World War I

9. _____

volunteer

10. _____

**Write the correct word from the box under each picture.**

| baseball | boxing | tennis |
| vacuum cleaner | washing machine |

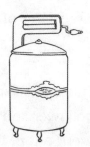

_____

_____

_____

_____

_____

**Write a sentence that tells how the above inventions and activities changed life in the Roaring Twenties.**

_____

_____

**Use the words in the box to fill in the blank lines in the paragraph.**

| Great Depression | loans | owner |
|---|---|---|
| sell | stock | drought |

Stocks are shares of companies. When you buy a company's stock, you become a part _____ of that company. On October 29, 1929 the stock market crashed. For several years, _____ prices had been rising. When stock prices began to fall, people were afraid of losing their money. Everyone tried to sell their stocks at the same time, making the prices go lower and lower. People lost their money and could not buy the things they needed. Stores went out of business because they could not _____ their goods. People lost their jobs and became unemployed. They could not pay their bank _____ and then banks went out of business too. To make matters worse, a severe _____ , or time of very little rain, in the Midwest led to giant dust storms, destroying thousands of farms. This bad time in American history is known as the _____ .

**Write a paragraph about what you think it might have been like to have lived during the time of the Great Depression.**

_____

_____

_____

_____

_____

_____

_____

_____

| **Home School Connection** | Have students read their paragraphs to a family member. Have them ask family members to tell them any stories they remember or have heard about the Great Depression. |
|---|---|

**Write a sentence using each word or phrase that tells about World War II.**

Pearl Harbor

1. _____

bomb

2. _____

fighting

3. _____

Hitler

4. _____

Japan

5. _____

Germany

6. _____

Nazi

7. _____

Holocaust

8. _____

concentration camp

9. _____

surrender

10. _____

Name

Five of the items in the box below were rationed in the United States during World War II. The other five items were built in factories – mostly by women who were taking the place of the men who were off to war. Put each item in the list in the correct box below.

| | | |
|---|---|---|
| bombers | uniforms | airplanes |
| gasoline | sugar | flour | meat |
| ships | parachutes | butter |

**Things Rationed**

_____

_____

_____

_____

**Things Built in Factories**

_____

_____

_____

_____

Write a paragraph that tells what things you might have done if you had been alive during World War II. Tell about the contribution you would have made to either rationing or manufacturing.

_____

_____

_____

_____

_____

**Home School Connection**

Ask students to share the information they have learned about World War II with a family member. They should ask the family member to share any additional information they might have or remember about World War II.

**Write a sentence using each word or phrase that tells about the United Nations.**

ambassador

1. _____

cooperate

2. _____

countries

3. _____

member

4. _____

New York City

5. _____

peace

6. _____

organization

7. _____

General Assembly

8. _____

international

9. _____

charter

10. _____

Name

**Read the following paragraph and answer the questions.**

The 1950s was an exciting decade – a ten-year period – for many Americans. The soldiers were back from World War II. People settled down and built new houses outside the cities in communities called suburbs. Many Americans bought television sets for entertainment and took vacations using the new interstate highways. Children played with new toys like hula hoops. People danced to the new sounds of rock and roll.

1. How long is a decade? _____

2. What kind of a decade was the 1950s? _____

3. Where did people build new houses? _____

4. How do you know that World War II was over? _____

5. What did many Americans buy for entertainment? _____

6. What was the name of the new highway system Americans used for travel? _____

7. What was one kind of new toy children played with in the 1950s? _____

8. What was a kind of new music that people danced to in the 1950s? _____

**Write a paragraph that compares what you have learned about life in the 1950s to life today.**

_____

_____

_____

_____

_____

_____

_____

_____

_____

**Home School Connection**

Ask students to share the information they have learned about the 1950s with a family member. They should ask the family member to share any additional information they might have or remember about the 1950s.

**Name**

Each of the words in the box is about something from space. Connect the word in the box to its matching picture. Then, beneath each picture, write a sentence about that picture.

_____

_____

astronaut
moon
space shuttle
satellite

_____

_____

_____

_____

_____

_____

**Home School Connection**

Have students share the information they have about space with a family member, naming the objects on this page and reading their sentences.

## Read the following paragraph and answer the questions.

The 1960s was a time of protest and change. America was involved in a controversial war, in Vietnam. Some people were in favor of the war; some people were against it. College students protested against the war with loud demonstrations. Farm workers protested their low wages and poor working conditions with boycotts. Native Americans demanded respect and the return of their land. Women demanded equal rights with men. African-Americans protested segregation and discrimination with peaceful sit-ins, in which people sit down in a place and refuse to leave. They demanded equal rights in schools, housing, and work. Dr. Martin Luther King, Jr. was a leader of the civil rights movement.

1. What kind of a decade was the 1960s? _____

2. With what country was America involved in a controversial war? _____

3. How do you know the war was controversial? _____

_____

4. Who protested the war? _____

5. Who protested their low wages and poor working conditions? _____

6. Who demanded respect and the return of their land? _____

7. Who demanded equal rights with men? _____

8. Who protested segregation and discrimination and wanted equal rights? _____

9. Who was a leader of the civil rights movement? _____

**Write the correct word from the box under each picture.**

| painter | dancer | photographer |
| :-: | :-: | :-: |
| sculptor | musician | |

_____

_____

_____

_____

_____

**Write a sentence using each word that tells about life in America today.**

mall

1. _____

computer

2. _____

diversity

3. _____

inventions

4. _____

nationalities

5. _____

contrasts

6. _____

culture

7. _____

downtown

8. _____

environment

9. _____

diversity

10. _____

In the space, draw a picture of an invention you would like to see created. Under the picture, write several sentences to describe your invention.

**Home School Connection**

Have students share their inventions with a family member. They should ask the family member to help them create another invention that would help around the home. Students' new drawings should be shared with the class.

Each of the words in the box is about Thomas Edison's invention, the light bulb. Connect the word in the box to its matching picture. Then, beneath each picture, write a sentence about that picture.

_____

_____

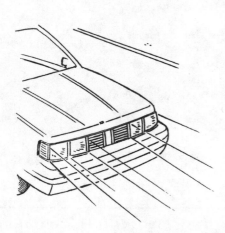

> headlights
> flashlight
> light bulb
> street light

_____

_____

_____

_____

**Home School Connection**

Encourage students to share the information they have learned about the invention of the electric light bulb with a family member, naming the objects on this page and reading their sentences.

Name

In the space below, draw a picture of at least three ways that people communicated before the invention of the telephone. Be sure to name each of the three ways.

On the lines below, write two sentences. The first should tell what you like most about having a telephone. The second sentence should tell what you like least about having a telephone.

_____

_____

_____

**Home School Connection**

Encourage students to ask a family member what they like most and what they like least about having or using the telephone. They should compare the family member's opinions with their own.

Imagine that you have been asked to come up with some ideas for a new kind of car. In the space below, list 10 things that are important for the outside of the car, and 10 that are important for the inside of the car. You may want to illustrate your new car on a separate sheet of art or drawing paper.

## My Ideas for a New Kind of Car

**The outside of the car would have:**

1. _____
2. _____
3. _____
4. _____
5. _____
6. _____
7. _____
8. _____
9. _____
10. _____

**The inside of the car would have:**

1. _____
2. _____
3. _____
4. _____
5. _____
6. _____
7. _____
8. _____
9. _____
10. _____

My new kind of car would sell for _____ .

The best thing about my new kind of car is _____ .

The colors that my new kind of car would come in are _____
_____ .

My new kind of car would be better than cars now because _____
_____ .

**Write a sentence using each word or phrase that tells about the camera.**

photographer

1. _____

develop

2. _____

film

3. _____

expose

4. _____

George Eastman

5. _____

lens

6. _____

light

7. _____

photography

8. _____

shutter

9. _____

pictures

10. _____

If you had to choose the programs that would be shown on television, what would they be? In the boxes below, write the names or descriptions of television programs that you would and would not broadcast.

## My Television Programming List

| The Programs I Would Broadcast | The Programs I Would Not Broadcast |
| --- | --- |
| 1. _____ | 1. _____ |
| 2. _____ | 2. _____ |
| 3. _____ | 3. _____ |
| 4. _____ | 4. _____ |
| 5. _____ | 5. _____ |
| 6. _____ | 6. _____ |
| 7. _____ | 7. _____ |
| 8. _____ | 8. _____ |
| 9. _____ | 9. _____ |
| 10. _____ | 10. _____ |

My all-time favorite television program is _____ .

The best thing about that program is _____ .

If I could choose new actors for that program, they would be _____
_____ .

The program I think should never be on television is _____
_____ .

**Home School Connection**

Encourage students to share their programming lists with a family member and compare their opinions.

**Name** _____

---

**Name**

Each of the words in the box is the name of a different kind of airplane. Connect the word in the box to its matching picture. Then, beneath each picture, write one way that kind of plane is used.

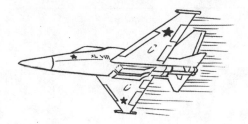

_____
_____

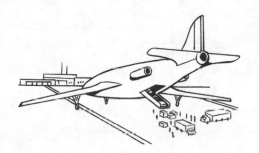

private plane
passenger jet
fighter jet
cargo plane

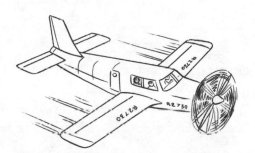

_____
_____

**Home School Connection**

Encourage students to share the information they have learned about airplanes with a family member, naming the objects on this page and reading the uses for each.

**Name**

## Write a sentence using each word or phrase that tells about the telescope.

Hubble Space Telescope

1. _____

moon

2. _____

planets

3. _____

Galileo

4. _____

Hale Telescope

5. _____

lens

6. _____

star

7. _____

sky

8. _____

image

9. _____

distant

10. _____

Have students read their sentences to a family member and share what they have learned about the telescope.

## Read the following paragraphs and answer the questions.

Before the invention of the printing press, all books were written one at a time, by hand. In ancient China, people first carved words into a block of wood, put ink on them, and pressed them against paper, but that was a very slow way to make a book. 1,000 years later, in 1456, when Johannes Gutenberg had an idea for using movable metal type, he changed forever how books were made.

Gutenberg's book was built by making letters one at a time and putting them together to make words.  When a whole page of words was ready, the letters had ink put on them. Then the letters covered in ink were pressed against a sheet of paper. When that page was printed, the letters would be used again to make a new page. Once all the pages were made, they were put together to make the new book.

## Number the steps below from 1 to 5 to show the correct order that Johannes Gutenberg used to make a book.

_____    The sheets of paper were put together to make a book.

_____    Ink was put on the letters.

_____    The letters were made.

_____    The letters were put together to make the words on a page.

_____    The letters with ink on them were pressed against a sheet of paper.

Name

Computers have made life different for people by helping them do things that were too difficult to do. But some things are still better not done by computer. On the lines below, make two lists. The first list should be things that are easier to do because of computers. The second list should be things that are just as easy to do without a computer.

**It is easier to do these things if you have a computer:**

1. _____
2. _____
3. _____
4. _____
5. _____
6. _____
7. _____
8. _____
9. _____
10. _____

**You don't really need a computer to do these things:**

1. _____
2. _____
3. _____
4. _____
5. _____
6. _____
7. _____
8. _____
9. _____
10. _____

**Home School Connection**

Encourage students to share their lists with a family member and compare their opinions.

**Write a sentence that describes each of the holidays below.**

Independence Day

1. _____

Memorial Day

2. _____

Labor Day

3. _____

Thanksgiving

4. _____

New Year's Day

5. _____

Hanukkah

6. _____

Christmas

7. _____

Cinco de Mayo

8. _____

Valentine's Day

9. _____

Kwanzaa

10. _____

**Home School Connection**    Have students read their sentences to a family member and share the what they have learned about holidays.

**Each of the words in the box is about Independence Day - the Fourth of July each year. Connect the word in the box to its matching picture. Then, beneath each picture, write a sentence about that picture.**

_____

_____

> fireworks
>
> picnic
>
> parade
>
> U.S. Flag

_____

_____

_____

_____

**Use the words or phrases below to write a sentence about George Washington.**

cherry tree

1. _____

president

2. _____

general

3. _____

honest

4. _____

War of Independence

5. _____

troops

6. _____

elected

7. _____

Mount Vernon

8. _____

Revolutionary War

9. _____

February

10. _____

**Home School Connection**     Have students read their sentences to a family member and share what they have learned about George Washington.

**Use the words or phrases above each line to write a sentence about Abraham Lincoln.**

log cabin

1. _____

theater

2. _____

assassinate

3. _____

Civil War

4. _____

freedom

5. _____

president

6. _____

slavery

7. _____

Lincoln Memorial

8. _____

North and South

9. _____

February

10. _____

**Home School Connection**

Have students read their sentences to a family member and share what they have learned about Abraham Lincoln.

**Use the words from the box to label the picture.**

|  |  |  |
| --- | --- | --- |
| corn | Mayflower | Pilgrims |
| pie | Native Americans | fish |

**Home School Connection**

Encourage students to share the information they have learned about Thanksgiving with a family member, using the picture on this page and the vocabulary words.

**Write several paragraphs about Martin Luther King, Jr., using all the words in the box below.**

| | | | |
|---|---|---|---|
| orator | freedom | dream | assassinate |
| march | speech | inequality | civil rights |
| racism | Nobel Prize | campaign | holiday |

_____

_____

_____

_____

_____

_____

_____

_____

_____

_____

_____

_____

_____

_____

_____

**Use the words or phrases below to write a sentence about Memorial Day.**

Decoration Day

1. _____

flowers

2. _____

died

3. _____

graves

4. _____

honor

5. _____

May

6. _____

veteran

7. _____

war

8. _____

memory

9. _____

Memorial Day

10. _____

**Home School Connection**    Have students read their sentences to a family member and share what they have learned about Memorial Day.

**Name**

**Write several paragraphs about Veteran's Day, using all the words or phrases in the box below.**

| | | |
|---|---|---|
| wreath | Arlington National Cemetery | truce |
| World War I | military | commemorate |
| November | U.S. Marine Corps War Memorial | |
| Tomb of the Unknowns | Armistice Day | flag |

_____

_____

_____

_____

_____

_____

_____

_____

_____

_____

_____

_____

_____

**Home School Connection**

Encourage students to share their paragraphs with a family member and get their reactions to their writing.

**Name** _____

Labor Day is celebrated each year on the first Monday in September. People in the United States and Canada use that day to honor working people. On the lines below, list 20 different kinds of jobs that working people have and a short description of each job.

1. _____
2. _____
3. _____
4. _____
5. _____
6. _____
7. _____
8. _____
9. _____
10. _____
11. _____
12. _____
13. _____
14. _____
15. _____
16. _____
17. _____
18. _____
19. _____
20. _____

**Home School Connection**

Encourage students to share their list with a family member and create together five more jobs with their descriptions to add to the list. Students should share their lists and additions with the class.

Name

Imagine that you are having a party to celebrate a personal, public, or national holiday. Use what you know and what you would like to fill in the information to plan your imaginary party.

### The food I will serve is:

_____

_____

_____

_____

_____

### This is what we will do at the party:

_____

_____

_____

_____

_____

### Please Come To My Party

We will celebrate _____

Please wear _____

We will eat _____

The place the party will be is _____

_____

The date of the party is _____

The party will start at _____

The party will end at _____

**Home School Connection**

Have students share their imaginary party plans with a family member. Encourage them to participate in planning a family event, if possible.

You have learned that America is a pluralistic society – a country of many cultures, religions, and languages. Use the words or phrases above each line to write a sentence about America's diversity.

culture

1. _____

diverse

2. _____

language

3. _____

multilingual

4. _____

pluralism

5. _____

religions

6. _____

diversity

7. _____

tradition

8. _____

travel

9. _____

unique

10. _____

**Home School Connection**

Have students read their sentences to a family member and share what they have learned about diversity in America.

**Using the information given in the box below, fill in the sentences about the Bill of Rights.**

---

### Guarantees from the Bill of Rights
### The First 10 Amendments to the U.S. Constitution

1st Amendment: Protects freedom of religion, speech, the press, and assembly.
2nd Amendment: Protects the right to bear arms; allows states to have an emergency army.
3rd Amendment: Protects people from having to house soldiers during peacetime.
4th Amendment: Protects people and their property from government searches without good reason.
5th Amendment: Sets up the grand jury; protects citizens against having to face trial more than once; guarantees due process.
6th Amendment: Guarantees fair and quick trial for an accused person.
7th Amendment: Guarantees a jury trial for court cases.
8th Amendment: Guarantees reasonable treatment and punishment for accused persons.
9th Amendment: Reserves for the people all rights not listed in the Constitution.
10th Amendment: Saves all other powers for the states and people.

---

1. The _____ Amendment protects a person's right to belong to any religious group they choose.

2. A person's right to a trial by jury is guaranteed by the _____ Amendment.

3. The _____ Amendment protects a person's house from being searched without a good reason.

4. The _____ Amendment guarantees that a person can't be tried more than once for the same crime.

5. A newspaper is guaranteed the right to print the news by the _____ Amendment.

6. The _____ Amendment forbids torture or unreasonable punishment.

7. A person's right to be a part of a protest march is guaranteed by the _____ Amendment.

8. The _____ Amendment guarantees anyone accused of a crime that they cannot be held in jail for a long period of time without a trial.

You have learned how our beliefs are alike and how they are different. In each box below, write a sentence telling why this belief might be important for you or anyone else in America.

**Friendship**

_____

_____

_____

_____

**Honesty**

_____

_____

_____

_____

**Love**

_____

_____

_____

**Respect**

_____

_____

_____

**Fairness**

_____

_____

_____

_____

**Tolerance**

_____

_____

_____

_____

**Home School Connection**

Have students share their sentences and opinions with a family member and solicit their opinions on the topic.

You have learned about America's diversity and the fact that not all people have the same opinion.  Use the words or phrases above each line pair to write one fact and one opinion.

**argument**

Fact _____

Opinion _____

**prejudice**

Fact _____

Opinion _____

**discrimination**

Fact _____

Opinion _____

**disagree**

Fact _____

Opinion _____

**solution**

Fact _____

Opinion _____

**Home School Connection**    Have students read their sentences to a family member.

Write a paragraph for each of the topics below.

### The Easiest Thing About Learning English

_____

_____

_____

_____

_____

### The Most Difficult Thing About Learning English

_____

_____

_____

_____

_____

**Home School Connection**    Encourage students to share their paragraphs with a family member and solicit their opinions on the topics.

America is a country where people enjoy all kinds of foods. Draw a picture of the food named in each box. Below the box, write a sentence that tells why you do or do not like that kind of food.

pizza

hamburger

taco

egg roll

**Home School Connection**

Have students share their drawings and opinions about the foods with a family member.

**Connect each word in List A to its opposite in List B. The first one is done for you.**

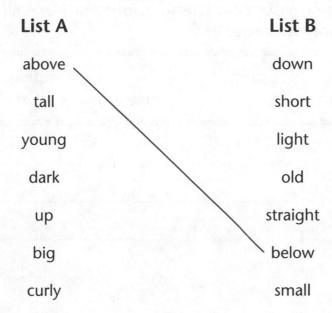

| List A | List B |
|--------|--------|
| above | down |
| tall | short |
| young | light |
| dark | old |
| up | straight |
| big | below |
| curly | small |

**Write a sentence for each pair of opposites. Circle the opposites in your sentence. The first one is done for you.**

1. *I looked (above) and (below) the table, but I still didn't find it.*

2. _____

3. _____

4. _____

5. _____

6. _____

7. _____

**Home School Connection**     Ask students to share their knowledge of opposites with a family member.

## 5.108  Name

Imagine that you have a new pen pal who you have never met. Write a letter to your pen pal that tells your new friend about you. Use all of the words from the box below in your letter.

> custom        native
> tradition        ancestor

_____

_____

_____

_____

_____

_____

_____

_____

_____

_____

_____

_____

_____

_____

**Home School Connection**

Have students ask a family member if they have ever communicated with a person they haven't met. Encourage students to listen to their family's experiences and share them with the class.

Use the word or phrase above each line to write a sentence that tells whether or not you might be interested in that hobby or activity.

dancing

1. _____

crafts

2. _____

sports

3. _____

music

4. _____

video games

5. _____

acting

6. _____

reading

7. _____

science

8. _____

history

9. _____

collecting

10. _____

**Home School Connection**

Encourage students to read their sentences and share their interests with a family member.

**Put a check mark (✓) in the box beside each word in the list that tells about a way people learn. Then, complete the sentences below the lists.**

☐ hear      ☐ memorize

☐ read      ☐ walk

☐ jump      ☐ slide

☐ practice      ☐ study

☐ call      ☐ write

☐ repeat      ☐ slow

☐ sing      ☐ learn

I learn best when _____

_____

_____

_____

It's hard for me to learn when _____

_____

_____

_____

In the Past box, write a word or phrase on each line that tells about you when you were five years old. In the Present box, write a word or phrase on each line that tells about you as you are now. Below each list, draw a sketch of what you looked like in the past and what you look like in the present.

| Past | Present |
| --- | --- |
| _____ | _____ |
| _____ | _____ |
| _____ | _____ |
| _____ | _____ |
| _____ | _____ |
| _____ | _____ |
| _____ | _____ |

**Home School Connection**

Encourage students to compare their thoughts about themselves both past and present with the thoughts of a family member.

**Write a short story about a family – either your family or an imaginary family. Use all the words in the box.**

| | | |
|---|---|---|
| family | aunt | brother |
| daughter | father | grandfather | cousin |
| mother | nephew | niece |
| sister | son | grandmother | uncle |

_____

_____

_____

_____

_____

_____

_____

_____

_____

_____

_____

_____

_____

You have learned how schools have changed over time. In each box, write a sentence related to the box topic that tells how schools are different today compared to 50 years ago.

books
_____
_____
_____

bus
_____
_____
_____

cafeteria
_____
_____
_____

desks
_____
_____
_____

pens
_____
_____
_____

computers
_____
_____
_____

**Home School Connection**   Have students share their sentences with a family member and solicit information on how schools have changed.

**Connect each word to its matching picture.**

skirt

suit

bathing suit

boots

pants

shirt

dress

coat

shoes

vest

You have learned that transportation has changed over time. Use the word above each sentence line to make a sentence that tells how transportation has changed. The first one is done for you.

buggy

1. *Long ago, you used a buggy to go shopping, but now we have cars.*

airplane

2. _____

boat

3. _____

bus

4. _____

car

5. _____

horse

6. _____

subway

7. _____

train

8. _____

wagon

9. _____

transportation

10. _____

In the space below, draw a map of a shopping center or mall you have visited. Label each store with the name of the store as well as the kinds of goods or services they sell. If you haven't visited a mall or shopping center, design one you would like to visit.

**Home School Connection**   Have students share their drawings with a family member and together check for accuracy in representing the mall or shopping center.

## Connect each word to its matching picture.

cellular phone
telephone
typewriter
computer
fax machine
letter

## Write a short paragraph using all the words in the box.

_____

_____

_____

_____

# 5.118

## Use the words in the box below to fill in the blank lines in the sentences.

| farmer | office | employee | career |
|---|---|---|---|
| employer | technology | salary | home |

1. Though many jobs have changed over time, one job that has been around for a long time is the job of a _____ since agriculture and food products are always needed.

2. If a person works with computers and computer related products, you could say that person works in _____ .

3. Technology and computers have made it possible for some people to do their work from _____ .

4. The person or company you work for is called your _____ .

5. If you work in an _____ , you usually work with a number of other people.

6. The job a person has chosen for his or her life's work is called a _____ .

7. The money you are paid for doing your job is called your _____ .

8. If you want to be a good _____ , you should be willing to work hard and do your best for your employer.

## Write a short paragraph describing the kind of job you think you might want to have.

_____

_____

_____

_____

_____

_____

**Home School Connection**

Have students share their paragraphs and get the advice and opinion of a family member on how best to pursue the student's chosen job.

You have learned that entertainment and play have changed over time. Look at the list below and put a check mark (✓) by the things that existed for entertainment 50 or 60 years ago when your grandparents were young.

☐ books ☐ board games

☐ television ☐ movies

☐ radio ☐ theater

☐ computer ☐ VCR

☐ videos ☐ telephone

☐ computer games ☐ video games

☐ CDs ☐ toys

Look at the items you checked in the list above. Imagine that these are the only means of entertainment and play for you. Write a paragraph describing what you think you might do on a Saturday at home if these items are your means of entertainment and play.

_____

_____

_____

_____

_____

_____

_____

**Home School Connection**

Have students share their lists and paragraphs with an older family member and discuss the differences in entertainment when the family member was the student's age.

You have learned that technology has changed over time. Above each numbered line is an example of technology that has been invented in the last 50 years. For each word, write a sentence that tells how our lives have changed because of that particular invention.

calculator

1. _____
_____

cellular phone

2. _____
_____

laptop computer

3. _____
_____

space shuttle

4. _____
_____

Hubble Telescope

5. _____
_____

**Which of the above inventions is the most important? Write a sentence that tells which is the most important and why you think it is the most important.**

_____
_____
_____
_____

**Home School Connection**

Encourage students to seek the opinion of a family member to find out which invention they feel is the most important and why.

**Name**

Put an ✗ over each lesson you have completed in Santillana Intensive English.

| Unit 1 | 5.1 | 5.2 | 5.3 | 5.4 | 5.5 | 5.6 | 5.7 | 5.8 | 5.9 | 5.10 |
|---|---|---|---|---|---|---|---|---|---|---|
| Unit 2 | 5.11 | 5.12 | 5.13 | 5.14 | 5.15 | 5.16 | 5.17 | 5.18 | 5.19 | 5.20 |
| Unit 3 | 5.21 | 5.22 | 5.23 | 5.24 | 5.25 | 5.26 | 5.27 | 5.28 | 5.29 | 5.30 |
| Unit 4 | 5.31 | 5.32 | 5.33 | 5.34 | 5.35 | 5.36 | 5.37 | 5.38 | 5.39 | 5.40 |
| Unit 5 | 5.41 | 5.42 | 5.43 | 5.44 | 5.45 | 5.46 | 5.47 | 5.48 | 5.49 | 5.50 |
| Unit 6 | 5.51 | 5.52 | 5.53 | 5.54 | 5.55 | 5.56 | 5.57 | 5.58 | 5.59 | 5.60 |
| Unit 7 | 5.61 | 5.62 | 5.63 | 5.64 | 5.65 | 5.66 | 5.67 | 5.68 | 5.69 | 5.70 |
| Unit 8 | 5.71 | 5.72 | 5.73 | 5.74 | 5.75 | 5.76 | 5.77 | 5.78 | 5.79 | 5.80 |
| Unit 9 | 5.81 | 5.82 | 5.83 | 5.84 | 5.85 | 5.86 | 5.87 | 5.88 | 5.89 | 5.90 |
| Unit 10 | 5.91 | 5.92 | 5.93 | 5.94 | 5.95 | 5.96 | 5.97 | 5.98 | 5.99 | 5.100 |
| Unit 11 | 5.101 | 5.102 | 5.103 | 5.104 | 5.105 | 5.106 | 5.107 | 5.108 | 5.109 | 5.110 |
| Unit 12 | 5.111 | 5.112 | 5.113 | 5.114 | 5.115 | 5.116 | 5.117 | 5.118 | 5.119 | 5.120 |

# Congratulations!

_____

has completed

**Santillana**
**INTENSIVE**
**English**

**5**

| Teacher | Date | | Parent | Date |

Este libro se terminó de imprimir en los talleres de
Panamericana Formas e Impresos S.A.
Calle 95 No. 95-28 Bogotá D.C.
Impreso en Colombia - Printed in Colombia